POETIC PRESCRIPTIONS
FOR
PLAGUING PROBLEMS

BIBLICAL REMEDIES
FOR WHEN LIFE BITES

KATHERINE NORLAND

Poetic
Prescriptions
Publishing

Poetic Prescriptions Publishing
Katherine Norland
PO Box 17033
Encino, CA 91416

© 2019 by Katherine Norland

All rights reserved.
No portion of this book may be stored in a
retrieval system, reproduced, or transmitted in
any form or by any means, except for brief
quotations in critical reviews or articles, without
the prior written permission of the author.

ISBN-13: 978-0-9983952-1-0

Photos and Cover Art: RT Norland
RobertNorland.com

Other titles written by Katherine Norland:

*Poetic Prescriptions for Eternal Youth:
Examining Earthly Beauty from a Heavenly
Perspective*

Poetic Prescriptions for Pesky Problems

For more information, please visit
PoeticPrescriptions.com.

POETIC PRESCRIPTIONS
FOR
PLAGUING PROBLEMS

BIBLICAL REMEDIES
FOR WHEN LIFE BITES

KATHERINE NORLAND

Acknowledgments

To my husband, **Rob**, thank you! Without your love, support, and understanding, my life would be much more challenging. In the sinking sand of this world, you are my rock. And thank you to my son, **Timothy**—you continue to teach me so much about what is important in life.

Thank you, **Donald** and **Arlene,** for your sacrifices to instill me with values, knowledge, and support in my creative endeavors.

Thank you to the many mentors I've had on my spiritual walk, who have consistently fed me with God's Word so that no matter what situation I found myself in, the Word would be what I could stand on. To my youth group teachers, **Pam** and **Bob Henkelman**, who planted the seeds; Pastor **Greg Stone**, who watered them; Pastors **Mel** and **Desiree Ayres,** who used the Word to prune me; and my spiritual mentor, **Mel Novak,** who continues to teach me to be bold for Christ.

Thanks to Actor/Director **Timothy Oman,** who pushes me in my acting and writing career to think outside the box and reach higher levels. And to **Kimberly Laux** for her feedback and calling me out when my words didn't match my intent.

Thank you, **Kim Shapiro, Monique Hester, LaQuesha Wiley**, and **Sheila Thompson,** for helping me build my dress for the cover art.

Most importantly, I am and will forever be grateful to the Almighty **God**, the Originator, Author, and Finisher of my faith, for getting me through all the difficult times in life, when it felt like pen and paper were my only outlets.

Contents

COMBAT: Armed with Pesticide,
Wearing a Flypaper Dress

ERADICATE: Time to Tent the House

Preface

I used to bottle up all my emotions and problems, until I was finally able to grab my pen and notebook and let them explode all over the paper. Poems focusing on my problems filled my notebooks. I'd lament and cry over how bad I thought my life was. I would reside in this funk, feeling like things would never get better.

I was depressed. From my perspective, it was true and justified because I believed I was such a failure. I wouldn't even begin anything because I already foresaw my defeat. I would let my hardships keep me down for so long that I had no clue how to escape this unhealthy mindset.

The more I grew in my relationship with God, the more I was able to see that for every problem I could face, God was the prescription. I learned that when He sent His Word to heal us, it was for any and every condition of the human spirit—body, mind, and soul. Suddenly, writing about my problems in life was only the beginning. It wasn't complete until I could find the prescription in God's Word for whatever ailed me. That is where the *Poetic Prescriptions* series began.

The responses I've gotten from my other *Poetic Prescriptions* books have made me realize that people crave to know how to be the kind of people God has called them to be—not only to live by the title of Christian but also to take on

Christ's nature and His authority that comes
with it.

Instead of letting ourselves be stopped by the
"life locusts" and the assaults that come our way,
we should conquer them. And after we've
conquered them, we are encouraged to lead
others out of the same pit that we've escaped
from.

In *Poetic Prescriptions for Plaguing Problems,*
I've taken the 10 plagues that the Egyptians faced
in the Bible (found in Exodus, chapters 7-12),
historical plagues like Black Death, the bubonic
plague, and others, and combined them with the
things that plague us now, such as thoughts of
divorce, obesity, fear, suicide, AIDS, domestic
violence, broken hearts, etc. Whether physical
ailments or broken spirits due to bad
relationships or poverty, I've written poetry that
will meet you right where you are.

I wrote this book to bring hope and courage to
those of you in need of direction, and to let you
know that we're in this together.

In the process of going through many of the
trials I write about in this book and finding the
Biblical solutions for them, I've learned to trust
God more and get closer to living the way He
wants me to live. My burdens have dropped, and
a joy and peace I hadn't experienced before, now
fills me.

I pray that reading this book will help you through whatever you're facing. And I hope that when your plaguing problems are conquered and you are victorious, you will lead others to the same prescription: the saving power of the Savior.

Introduction

When I put this book together, I laid it out in such a way that the effects of my problems lessen as the book progresses. Not that what I was dealing with was less offensive or heartbreaking, but rather, they became easier to manage as I built my knowledge and my relationship with God.

In the first section of this book, titled "The Plague: It's Like a Locust Infestation," you'll find poems about these "locusts":

- **Addiction.** Even though a substance or person is harmful to you.
- **Domestic Violence.** The need to break the chain.
- **Helping Others.** Even when you're afraid or have nothing left to give.
- **Lust.** How it seeps in and takes over your thoughts.
- **Disapproval from Others.** When they don't understand the calling in your life.
- **The Misery of Selfishness.** How indifference to others can blind you.
- **Disobedience.** How the decisions you make affect your children.
- **Suicide.** Be reassured that you're not alone and that God can turn things around if you give Him a chance.

In section two, "Aware: Place Roach Motels in Every Room," you'll read poems about these plaguing problems:

- **Self-Abuse.** When you've done wrong and can't forgive yourself.
- **Being a Workaholic.** Are you chasing the right thing?
- **Sensing Negative People.** How to get them out of your life.
- **Marriage Challenges.** Is it time to divorce or focus on their positive traits?
- **Obesity.** How does it affect your witness within the Church?
- **Freedom through Obedience to God.** Even when it doesn't make sense.
- **Poverty.** Is your mindset keeping you from an abundant life?
- **AIDS.** Living with a death sentence.

In section three, "Combat: Armed with Pesticide, Wearing a Flypaper Dress," I'll share these remedies with you:

- **Self-Forgiveness.** Forgiving yourself for your past.
- **Whining.** How complaining is just the trash that lures the Father of Flies in.
- **Trusting God.** Tithing, giving, and putting Him first.

- **Challenges.** Ridding problematic cobwebs from your life before the spiders eat you alive.
- **Prayer.** When all looks hopeless.
- **Rejection.** When those who are supposed to love you, don't.
- **Persecution.** When you leave your former way of life to go the godly route.
- **Complacency.** Becoming like the walking dead.

In the final section of the book, "Eradicate: Time to Tent the House," you'll explore these prescriptive poems:

- **Idolatry.** Is this why your life isn't going as planned?
- **Celebrating Always.** Not letting temporary trials on Earth steal our joy.
- **Love for God's Word.** How the Scriptures can ignite you.
- **Witnessing.** When you feel inept at sharing God's Word.
- **Miracles.** Does God still perform them?
- Learning to Sail Again. After your life has been shipwrecked by molestation.
- **Crying Out to God.** When you have nothing left and no idea what to pray for.
- **Your Calling.** Is it tied to something you hate?
- **Trust.** How to make it through when it looks impossible.

THE PLAGUE

It's Like a Locust Infestation

Addiction

I'm dangerously close to you;
You're still this user's drug of choice.
Though I attempt to shout you out,
I'm silenced, strung out on your voice.
Ashamed my psyche took a hit;
This jonesing wildcat has lost it.
An intervention would be fit,
`Cause I don't know how else to quit.

Resisting's hollow; I've no might.
My killer is my appetite.
I'm not addicted; it's not true.
I've just not had enough of you.

I know together we're no good,
Yet in denial I could be.
No twelve-step tango calms my mind;
Your poison has a hold on me.
I must inhale when you get close;
Your vapor leaves me comatose.
I'm hazed each time I take your dose;
My negligence is more than gross.

Resisting's hollow; I've no might.
My killer is my appetite.
I'm not addicted; it's not true.
I've just not had enough of you.

I've lost my manners, can't behave,
No iron will to drop this dope.
Spun outta sight, I've had my fix.
When dry, I search for antidote.

If honey bee would hunt for vein,
Your venom stings would numb the pain.
The buzz wears off and I'm not sane;
The hook of ecstasy's to blame.

Resisting's hollow; I've no might.
My killer is my appetite.
I'm not addicted; it's not true.
I've just not had enough of you.

My stomach's pumped; I'm drunk on coal.
I'm choked and chained to metal slab.
Can't worry `bout a relapse now,
Stone sober in a cold rehab.
Can't shut my ears and run away;
It's to your siren I am prey.
I can't detox if you do stay,
But one day at a time, I pray.

Resisting's easier with God's might;
It kills unholy appetites.
I'm not addicted; it's not true.
My remedy's to change my view.

Nightshades

I want to rid the dead in me,
Uncover hidden bones.
Blot out bad memories for good,
Of these abject tombstones.

My rotting corpse just won't stay down;
I hide what I fear most.
But worms crawl in and out of me;
My carcass is compost.
I've read old things have passed away;
This creature's become new.
Then why do I react this way,
Abhorring what I do?

Was it my torment as a child?
Is that where trauma's traced?
Yet other dangers were put down,
Lie dead where they were placed.

I don't want me to be like this;
Take haste to break this curse.
I can't control myself, I fear;
I don't want to get worse.
I'm lashing out at those I love
Because of my short fuse.
There's no excuse to hit when mad
Just `cause I was abused.

Need bad-behavior beetles bombed
To leave them all behind.
I want to harvest fruit that heals,
Not hogweed that will blind.

I thought my past was one I tilled.
Why is the ground still hard?
I need to propagate new crops
That bring life to my yard.
Can't stunt gross growth if fertilized;
It won't die but persist.
Nor have a great relationship
Expressed with angry fist.

You see, my field is overgrown;
It's full of rocks and grim.
If I want topiary here
It takes more than a trim.

So why do I memorialize
My damage done when young?
I realize too late that what
Was planted has now sprung.
Then when my wrath can't be contained
I rage since I've been hurt.
Make those around me cower in fear;
They're put on high alert.

There's abrin in my poisonous deeds
Sprout castor beans, foxglove.
I serve these rosary pea seeds.
Nightshades kill those I love.

Resigned, I lay; worms feast on me.
I'm overcome by fears.
Yet You revive me from the dead,
Plants watered with my tears.
You've pruned all toxins from my leaves
And plucked each deadly weed.

I'll never sow a stinging tree
Or cause someone to bleed.

With You beauty and life spring forth;
I make amends for what I've done.
What blooms now can revive and heal;
No weeds can overrun.

Can't Look Them in the Eye

God gave me much to do,
And yet my hands are tied.
With many lepers' needs,
My prayers and tears collide.

      It seems that most don't care;
      They see outcasts and scoff.
      They don't want to be near
      When parts of them fall off.

But me? I say kind words,
Like "Be warm!" and "Be filled!"
Yet I don't meet their needs,
So that their storm is stilled.
I don't have cash to give;
Air hugs make them morose.
They've trails of crusty skin;
I cannot get too close.

      But I'll drive by and pray
      Right here at a safe distance
      Till I have means to give
      Some tangible assistance.

I need to be like Christ,
But I'm not that courageous.
Why should I get so close?
I dread their fate's contagious!
Can't look them in the eye
Or put their fears at ease.
Can't cure their colonies;
I have no expertise!

Yet God's my healing salve
For all hang-ups I have
If His love's what I share
Then they will know I care.

Locust Lust

Goodbye, my lust, it's time to go,
Refuse to let these feelings show.
Heart races when I think of you;
We can't be: I tell me, "We're through."

I fantasize, and I like that,
But caving in, I would fall flat
Onto my face. Who'd pick me up?
My spouse might come to interrupt—

While we profess our love is true.
Can't take that risk. What would we do?
Would you live up to what's imagined?
Or would my daydreams lose their passion?

Goodbye, my lust, I should not stay;
You're getting close, must go away.
Illusions get the best of us;
Submit to my unholy lusts.

Pretending can't go on like this;
Can't give in to a single kiss.
If our lips met, we'd escalate.
We'd go too far; lust turned to hate.

Beguiled by you, I thought it fate;
I didn't lock my garden's gate.
I gave you reign to just fly in;
So fragrant is forbidden sin.

You raid me like a rampant storm,
Like locust infestations swarm.
Temps rise, pulse rapid, hard to breathe;
Sans touch you're penetrating me.

Not normal, now I am consumed,
To taste your appetite; I'm doomed.
Can I save my endangered crop?
Let's stop, so stop, must stop, now stop!

Retreat! Don't kill what I should keep,
But any harvest left, you eat.
How can I just get rid of you?
Confessing what I know is true.

I'm loved. I need no other mate;
Contrary thoughts I'll fumigate.
Pride lost, I cry, reach out and yelp
With burning branches beg for help.

No mooning over what lures me;
When I resist, grasshoppers flee.
Protect my pledge, it's not that hard
When I zap locusts from my yard!

You Want Me Quarantined

Defend myself? I don't have to,
To you or anyone.
From your reaction, it seems like
You've toxic-shock syndrome.
You tell me that I don't fit in,
That there's no place for me,
But members that appear as weak
Still have necessity.

You say I'm not presentable,
Must hide behind closed door
Yet body parts that we protect
Then prove they're honored more.
Some parts we keep from public view,
Yet they're not to be scorned.
Some people that are not like you,
In heaven most adorned.

God's bod should not divide itself;
If suffering, give care.
So too if parts are honored, then
In unity be there.
You cannot understand my acts;
You think that I'm a fiend.
Of what I do, you don't approve.
You want me quarantined?

You don't know what my motives are
Or know of my intent.
So to conclusions quick you jump,
Assume I must repent.

You don't know what I'm called to do;
It's not the same for everyone.
Be wary of your own Earth walk;
We all will answer to the Son.

You're frightened what I do
Will have the power to go systemic.
I really hope you're right;
I'd love to see it go pandemic.
So thanks for your concern;
I'm liable for what I do.
However, F.Y.I.,
I'm not accountable to you.

We're part of the same body, yes?
No part should subjugate.
The stomach cannot be the king;
The eyes should not dictate.
Let's trust the brain to lead us right;
It will not cause us harm.
The hip has no room to decide
What happens with the arm.

What I do makes no sense to you,
For you have your own aim.
God gives to each his own life's work
And no one's is the same.
I can't do what you do;
It's not how I'm designed.
Let's in conjunction work;
The outcome might align.

Let's calibrate what we do best,
Be sharpened and acute,
Not fuss about how other parts
Will choose to execute.
What's critical for you
May not be part of my decree.
If doing what you ought
You'd have no time to fret `bout me.

The best thing we could do right now:
Choose love as our default
And work together, not be quick
In launching an assault.

Dark Misery Longs

I've never pitied slaves and how they rush
To their crude huts, whilst I in palace plush.
And yet in truth those poor were better slept;
I tossed and turned from promises unkept.
No feelings for their comfort, my soul charred;
With each decision made, my heart grew hard.

Then darkness came and made itself well-known;
It stretched its full self over windows shown.
Through blackened days and nights, I cannot see
Nor feel when numbness all but covers me.

There is no sustenance within my scope;
Now I'm the prisoner who has no hope.
My servants fled, none here to make my bread.
My stomach growls; in days I may be dead.
I hear slave children squealing with delight,
But have no joy myself since I've lost sight.

I've heard some sense when love is in the air;
I pose my arms to hug, but no one's there.
I stand alone and cold; the outlook's bleak.
Not finding happiness in what I seek.

Could signs like these then be a miracle?
Is darkness that enclaves me spiritual?
When I admit my need for help, clouds lift;
My problems suddenly begin to shift.
Then three days in I got another chance
To lean towards God or keep my evil stance.

When I release traditions from my past,
My startling view is new and unsurpassed.
I step into my future; all feels right,
Surrounded by the warmth of wondrous light.

And what deific voice bids me to "Come"?
Though I'd ignored His whispers from day one
Here, captured in His boundless love, I muse.
Why had I been so stubborn with my views?
I thought that I knew better; I was wrong.
I was the one who made my misery long.

Who Said You're Naked?

I was mere dust; You gave me life
    And placed me on Your level ground.
Desired to give me everything,
    You made me Eve so I'd abound.

    In garden's paradise we've all
        Free reign, save for a single tree.
    We see You bid for us to come.
        You dangle life's eternal key.

In Your direction we draw near;
    We know You are the only way.
We don't know there's an enemy
    That wants to coil us 'round like prey.

    Oh, God, Your whisper captivates,
        But then we feel we'd be remiss
    To not check out this stunning snake,
        Receive his mesmerizing hiss.

He tells us how to be like You,
    And that would be our sole delight.
We see the fruit is good for food;
    Voraciously we take a bite.

    Now good and evil both revealed,
        Henceforth our innocence is killed.
    Just realizing that we're nude
        Has left our fig-leaf diaper filled.

Amidst the cool of day, we hear
    You, in the garden, call our name.
Sin realized, regret does rise;
    Outlaws of paradise, ashamed.

    Here forced to work by sweat of brow
        To make the savage garden grow.
    Contend with nascent breeds of weed
        Before invention of the hoe.

My partner in the crime wails out,
    Death screams crescendo, birthing pain.
New sinful nature does descend
    When we give birth to our son Cain.

    Each generation takes a step
        Toward more righteousness—or not
    As they pursue their parents' cue
        To run to God—or not get caught.

Our firstborn is a vagabond;
    He couldn't keep envy from his eye.
His barren heart and rage had made
    Our second first on Earth to die.

    Our kin will emulate our life,
        And often take it one step further.
    So will we live in wickedness—
        Or serve our God with faith and fervor?

Each time we act, we train our child;
    Be mindful of each move we make.
Our words ignored for action's sake,
    Not just our life, but theirs at stake.

The Ledge

Such fluffy clouds hang in the sky;
The temperature's just right.
I see her standing near the ledge
Like she's been there all night.
Wind whips her hair across her face
Like tissue, dries her tears.
She stands deliberating life,
Steps to the edge with fear.

"Step back!" I shout. You shouldn't jump;
That's not the best way out.
We cannot hear a silent cry;
You're going to have to shout!
You can't see what the future holds;
It hides behind a hedge.
But past it something better waits;
It's time to leave the ledge.

It isn't easy; that I know.
No one alleged it'd be.
Of all that's wrong, thoughts fly like birds;
Their droppings all you see.
I'm telling you they'll take off soon;
The nest they built won't last.
You will be able to move on
Not trapped inside the past.

Your trials blow like wind; pressures build.
Stand firm against the breeze.
Windbreaker coats won't keep you safe.
Step down! I'm begging, please!

The howling wind is far too much;
Of course you've lost your poise.
Yet crowds below think it's an act;
Their gossip's clanging noise.

They whisper, "What is wrong with her?"
They honk and sirens blare.
But they've no clue what you've been through,
So they just point and stare.
Rain pounds from clouds on every side;
You've held on through cyclones.
But call for help when flocks dive-bomb;
You can't fight fowl alone.

Persuaded you're their target now,
No matter what I say.
But you can't see a thing at all,
Eyes homed on yesterday.
Through this torment your faith has failed.
You can't forget what's done.
Abuse yourself and won't forgive.
Why see tomorrow's sun?

Discouraged and you're overwhelmed,
The clouds of life too thick.
But hope deferred's the very thing
That makes your heart feel sick.
Your wish for death is justified;
You say you will not try.
But wind and birds cannot be blamed
If you decide to die.

In trials your patience has been pecked;
Faith's tested when you bleed.
But patience has its perfect work,
Lacks nothing that you need.
If you need wisdom for this task
So you don't cause you harm,
God liberally gives to all who ask
So jump into His arms.

The wind will stop and birds will flee,
Although you don't know how.
Please step back and evaluate.
I've been where you are now:
Considering my worth in life,
Tiptoes pushed past the edge.
When I cried out, God sent me help,
And swooped me from the ledge.

AWARE

Place Roach Motels in Every Room

Bashing My Head Against the Wall

I was insensitive and rude,
But it's already done.
I flog myself repeatedly,
And ripped flesh is no fun.

I've messed up royally, again,
But, then, that's nothing new.
I've eaten holes in your good clothes,
Nary a moth in view.

Quick to assume and end up wrong,
Which leaves some folks offended.
My spirit's grieved, so I must get
The God connection mended.

At times I've filled up pails with tears
When envy has grown strong.
I've maimed myself too frequently;
I punish me when wrong.

I won't keep crawling on the ground,
And let the devil win.
Or have him puff me up with pride,
Then pop when pricked by sin.

I'm like a maggot when he taunts;
I feast on feces' guilt,
Or like a snail that's crushed its shell
And cannot be rebuilt.

"You idiot!" I call myself
And other ruthless names.
I bash my head against the wall
For causing people pain.

Perhaps I'll calm my manic ways
So I can be more docile.
Am I a better witness if
I'm still, encased in fossil?

I squash myself just like a pest
Under condemning shoes.
Can't bring atoning gifts to God
Without the Bible's cues.

If I've offended, go to them,
And settle ere to court.
God won't accept my sacrifice
If it's His will I thwart.

I'll break regret and make amends,
Just like the Lord's advised.
Can't go to God if I've hurt them
And I don't apologize.

Since my obedience brings grace,
I'm not seen as a gnat.
I won't berate myself if I've
Sincerely done just that.

When knowing that I've grieved someone,
I'll take it to the Lord.
And make sure that I walk the steps
It takes to be restored.

For kindness trade my flogging tools,
And stop my self-assaults
If they won't budge and hold a grudge
Then I won't be at fault.

When I've obeyed and carried out
Each thing God said to do
Then by the Father I'm absolved
No matter what they choose.

If they hate how I buzz around
I will not clip my wings.
I'll smell the flowers and lift my mood,
And try hard not to sting.

Chasing Scraps

Am I convinced that all the work I do
Will bless mankind and be fulfilling too?
But workaholics like me live by "shoulds,"
Not pausing to enjoy life's greater goods.

Days spent in search of gold in garbage heaps,
Accomplishing the nothing that's for keeps.
I'm overzealous; that's my earnest fault,
But not productive, reaping real results.

The more
I fall
Behind
My work and goals,
The more
My plan's
Been ravaged,
Swiss-cheese holes.

And still I travel to the same old place,
Though not rewarded in this ceaseless chase.
This rodent's maze is nothing but a tease,
When I get to the end, there is no cheese.

Adventure's lost when living life by rote.
No power in my praise or Bible quote.
I glance at Scriptures fast; away I speed.
But if I sought God first, He'd meet my need.

I make
A list
Of tasks

I can't get done.
I work
Long hours
Far past
The setting sun.

With slow momentum, I've not made a dime.
Am I convinced it will pay off in time?
But I've no guarantee it will work out.
I'll push down thoughts I fear to think about.

Why rest? My runner's high is fuel for zeal;
I don't believe I'm on a hamster wheel.
I'll let endorphins cover up my rage;
I won't concede I'm trapped inside a cage.

I'm Satan's pet;
I'm brought
To show
and tell.
Don't know
That I'm
in my own
Private hell.

I spin; I toil; I wear myself so thin.
Six hours sleep, then do it all again!
Don't notice that the view has never changed;
I churn the same old whey 'til I'm deranged.

Won't take advice, 'cause I've no time to hear.
Can't stop; I'll lose the ground I'm holding dear.
It seems that only God can change my ways;
With Him I'd get my cheese and leave the maze.

My body
Tires out
And I
Collapse;
Look up
To see
I'd just been
Chasing scraps.

They Just Wanna Fight

False friends possess opinions sure,
Like roaches probing my behavior.
Speak horribly regarding me,
Such as, "She could not love the Savior."
    `Cause repercussions from my past
    At last revealed my sins were vast.
    They find my faults and are aghast;
    They birth them out like eggs, so fast —

That I can't get a word in, to
Defend the point of view I see.
They couldn't care less to hear my side;
They're so convinced that they know me.
    I wonder what's attracted them.
    To these attacks, I'm a beginner.
    I've never seen such hunger here.
    Perhaps to them I smell like dinner.

These dark deeds they deduce I do,
So odious they think I am,
Are sewage that they dine upon.
When I flip on the light, they scram!
    When I mess up, they point it out;
    They teach their nymphs what they surmise.
    These omnivores have their own flaws,
    But hard shells are a proud disguise.

Depict themselves a certain way,
And then before I know, they molt.
They look to multiply themselves;
With orange oil I will revolt.

I won't let what they speak of me
Get me depressed or shut me down.
They're in the trade of finding fault,
With every seeker in this town.

They crawl all over picnic plans
They're swimming in my lemonade.
Bug bombs I pitch with fervent clip
Like anti-parasite grenades.
    In darkened crevasses they hide
    And leave their droppings everywhere.
    All joy I had is squeezed from me
    When they accuse me and compare.

I rack my brain. Might I be wrong?
I question if I'm living right,
Examining myself too long,
It hit me: they just wanna fight.
    Won't listen to them list each glitch;
    I'll plug my ears before they start.
    I won't tune in to lies they snitch;
    It's God who sees inside my heart.

So I'll debug, get rid of them,
Place roach motels in every room.
Removing every trace of hate,
Their sabotage I will entomb.
    Now I'll protect the space I'm in,
    Seal every opening and dent,
    Oust hypocrites who feed on me,
    Who've signed no lease and pay no rent.

For Better or Worse

For Worse:

Although we're skin on skin, I'm still alone,
In solitary, sick, confined at home.
With fever, chills, and weakness, I face doom;
Wed to my barf bag, no sign of my groom.

Projectile vomiting my insides out,
But you don't hear me even when I shout.
You wonder why I'm sorta-kinda miffed.
You loved me once. So did your feelings shift?

I'm faced now with estrangement and rejection
Like I've attracted some flea-borne infection.
When did your blushing bride become a hag
Avoiding me like I'm bubonic plagued?

You press in deep, inflaming my buboes.
Won't nurse my hurt, but that's the way it goes.
With blind eyes, misinterpret all my pain;
You cannot cope with your agenda slain.

Out in your man cave, clueless and serene,
Donned headphones so you cannot hear me scream.
'Til death do us then part, so much at stake.
Will we survive this virulent outbreak?

Both caught up, self-absorbed by our own tasks,
Dismissing each request the other asks.
In desperate need, yet our behavior mocks;
You watch tutorials while I sort out socks.

No nudge felt in the spirit we've repressed,
With all the things that matter not addressed.
Have we forgotten vows of better/worse?
So with mascara tears, my answer's terse.

Death penalty's no threat; communicate!
Our actions scream that we should separate.
We've put a wall across our countryside.
With barriers, we've no chance to collide.

Your work comes first and I am pushed aside.
Today is Christmas Day. Why would you hide?
No mistletoe to kiss `neath; you shoot missiles.
Let me bedeck your bed in thorns and thistles.

I need a bullhorn; you can't take a hint.
Remember me? I'm not your pocket lint!
An act of parliament can't axe our ways.
Without a cure, I've only scant few days.

You see, I'm sick; my skin's turned black and blue.
My blood's been poisoned. Now what will you do?
My heart feels like it's died a violent death,
'Cause you say, "Wait," but I can't hold my breath.

Must clean the air before I soon relapse.
My oxygen's cut off; my lungs collapse.
This plague is killing me, yet you still doubt.
Excuse my messy moments bleeding out.

For Better:

Back from the dead, I've had some time to think.
A marriage to another'd still be kinked.
So iron sharpens iron; I've seen that's true.
Perhaps at times I use mine to poke you.

And you leave yours to lie 'round so I trip;
You leave me on the ground with broken hip.
Your crassness and neglect, they still don't work,
But...I can't live with any other jerk.

Body Mass Index

Obesity inside the church has gained,
And yet the sum of membership is light.
Ignoring elephants within the room,
I've met pre-Christians turned off at our sight.

To them, outside appearance counts the most;
Our insides, they don't judge as thoroughly.
Although we know that it's our spirit man
That holds the key to our eternity.

On Earth we tend to judge books by their covers,
Assessments made by how someone appears.
If we are sloppy, floppy, and unkempt,
It closes up their minds and hearts to hear.

The taut, the toned, the trim oft times tune out
When doughy Butterballs point out their sin.
Why follow one who's winded climbing stairs,
Whose fastest gait is but to waddle in?

We feign concern about our B.M.I.
And true, those stats have been left in the lurch.
The doctor wants us in a healthy range,
Yet let's not slight the Index of the church.

Consumed with filling up our empty parts,
But when we solely dwell on our inside,
We congregate where we are comfortable.
We don't reach out to those in need, outside.

We have an epidemic in our church,
Though it's within our hearts to do good deeds.
We want to help those starving in the world
But feel we're powerless with all their needs.

Could feed an army with the scraps we've left,
When we hold chicken dinners, grabbing funds.
But if we had allotted cash to give,
The starving would be fed, not us rotund.

Those people perfect outwardly won't hear
That there's a "better" way from squishy saints.
That God improves each area of life,
When it looks obvious we've no restraints.

We have free will to eat what we do please.
Our souls are saved no matter what our size.
But could we give more thought to what we chew
To harvest mankind, God's most costly prize?

In Heaven there'll be time for us to feast.
On Earth let's tighten up our belts and fast.
If it could help us with our witness here,
In gathering the souls of men at last.

If we know it's the lost we want to win,
Then let's put down the steak and butter knife.
Because most aren't convinced the portly can
Shed light on dropping baggage in their life.

Freedom's Not Born but Taken

We'll ask our captors for their goods,
But will Egyptians give or hold?
This plan for freedom makes no sense
That they'll give raiment, jewels, and gold.

My neighbor shared my growing qualms;
We feared to kill our best of flock.
I told him if we trust in God
His orders won't come back to mock.

But clearly he did not believe
Jehovah God would harm his kid.
Because he is an Israelite,
Thought he'd be safe if he just hid.

The dark Egyptian night was rising;
We warned our Nile-eyed friend beware,
And use the blood from perfect lambs
Then all our firstborn will be spared.

At home I struggled with my doubts.
This lamb I can't afford to lose.
But if I kill it—God will save?
He'll know that it's His will I choose.

If not, my wife could not recoup;
Our firstborn is her life and breath.
Must sacrifice our livelihood
So we'll prevent our namesake's death.

So solidly my feed should stand;
God's pledge to me's a sturdy rock.
Yet I'm concerned about my stash
Of treasures; I have taken stock—

Of what I have and what I lack,
And what I want to have more of.
Don't think God's plan will give me mine;
There're things I need beyond just love.

Some say that I'm hard headed, true.
I've also seen nine plagues go by.
It's not that I require more proof;
Sometimes it's painful to comply.

I've seen destruction from God's hand,
Fear for my first I'll have no more.
In case I erred and missed the mark,
Applying lamb's blood `round our door.

Don't kill my child, for we are Yours;
No one escapes, not bird nor beast.
Don't want our eldest youth to die.
I've trust issues, to say the least.

Remember, I'm an Israelite.
Your wrath will fall from king to slave.
Don't bring on me Egyptians' curse.
It's You who saves us from the grave.

So slowly midnight's come and gone,
With it I let my angst release.
I questioned Your protection. Why?
I oft let Pharaoh steal my peace.

Just then I heard my neighbor scream;
He wailed like I'd not heard before.
I knew right then God kept His word;
His will performed and nothing more.

We grabbed our things and headed out.
Egyptian friend called to my wife.
Profusely hugged and thanked us both;
Advice from us saved her son's life.

And now for us our freedom's born;
Our slavery's dead and will not haunt.
With arms upraised we leave this place
With riches that surpassed our want.

Still Think I Stink

And like the Moscow plague and riot
    Of seventeen seventy-one,
The tumult's not a cinch to face
    When my well-being's on the run.

Authorities wish I'd believe
    That their restraints are not that bad.
That dwelling on eternal hope
    Should be enough to make me glad.

Mundane dilemmas like cold baths
    Have caused me anger, fear, alarm.
But if I would believe Your Word,
    Those false emotions would disarm.

Now they've destroyed my property;
    Yet time would make it fade away.
I'm not repaid for what they break;
    Yet years would crumble it like clay.

And why on Earth do I obsess
    About what others seem to think?
'Cause even if I caused world peace,
    Some people would still think I stink.

I own no house; I've lost my job.
    Yet family and friends love me.
Why linger on the lack of food?
    This ain't how it will always be.

I riot in the streets and beg;
    I rail, complaining of my lack.
I make demands, but only You
    Can take suppression off my back.

They've cut the tang down from my bell,
    So it's in silence that I cower.
I'm just a useless metal hunk,
    So now remove me from this tower.

The money's gone before the month;
    I'm stuck in squalor with great need.
What'd help me more than anything
    Is for my mindset to be freed.

Distressed by such frivolity
    That will with age just pass away—
Deprives me of the gift You gave,
    This precious present wrapped today.

After the Fall

How can you say to take it slow?
There're places that I wanna go.
I have no clue how I'll get there;
But let's find out, and load for bear.

I don't know who my parents are,
If dead or eating caviar.
But either way I'd not fit in,
Or lose the need for medicine.

When school chums run from me, I'm blamed,
No way to talk about my pain.
Rejected every time I tried,
My diagnosis is denied.

Am I invisible? I guess.
They won't confront what I address.
Regime says AIDS does not exist.
Eyes closed, they can't see what they've missed.

I'm learning how to live, although exiled;
I'm that forgotten face of love's lost child.
My hope's not shattered; I will make it work.
Won't pick at wounds from unintended hurt.
I'll piece my life together; I won't hide.
My load feels lighter when you're by my side.

I tried my best to not get caught,
Took pills while stomach's tied in knots.
My teacher found me sneaking meds;
Throughout the whole of school, word spread.

When I came near, in fear kids ran;
They were too scared to hold my hand.
They wouldn't give a single glance,
So I was forced to give up dance.

My prayers that I could ever have
Relationships' consoling salve
Wiped out by those who do not care,
As they pretend that I'm not there.

Was told that there's a "No AIDS rule."
The teachers kicked me out of school
`Cause kids had parents who complained.
And I was never so ashamed.

I'm learning how to live, although exiled;
I'm that forgotten face of love's lost child.
My hope's not shattered; I will make it work.
Won't pick at wounds from unintended hurt.
I'll piece my life together; I won't hide.
My load feels lighter when you're by my side.

I've animals that do their part,
That I can love, yet save my heart.
To not infect, I'd rather flee.
The human beast strays far from me.

To have a family's far-fetched,
Yet my imagination stretched.
To live a full life is my quest,
Yet I am hesitant, at best.

I've heard that infants won't stay `live
If they're not held; they cannot thrive.
And I too crave that fleshly touch,
Require embracing just as much.

I must live fast, intense, and strong,
`Cause death awaits and won't be long.
Won't reach my dreams if I don't try.
I'll say hello before goodbye.

I'm learning how to live, although exiled;
I'm that forgotten face of love's lost child.
My hope's not shattered; I will make it work.
Won't pick at wounds from unintended hurt.
I'll piece my life together; I won't hide.
My load feels lighter when you're by my side.

Poet's Note: I was inspired to write the poem
"After the Fall" in response to the true account
of the young adults who contracted pediatric
AIDS, through no fault of their own, during the
Romanian AIDS crisis of the 1990s. To see the
documentary AFTER THE FALL: WHEN HIV
GROWS UP, you may visit the website at
www.afterthefallfilm.com.

COMBAT

Armed with Pesticide, Wearing a Flypaper Dress

Struggling Against Myself

I want to hear God's words;
I need mine to be fewer.
Must barbecue my flesh
`Til holy, seared on skewer.

Hard heart, skin burns, soul strives;
What's right I yearn to do.
And yet my flesh gets stuck
To feeble things like glue.
These plagues that God put forth
Renewed backslidden faith
But not 'til after loss
Did I seek out God's face.

I had succumbed to kings
Whose power seemed so great,
But when magicians came,
Their wands could not abate.

Their false and evil power
Couldn't stop what God released.
Dark bruises dress my flesh;
Unclean are man and beast.
I know I had been warned.
Why couldn't I just be loyal?
Didn't think this plague would hit;
I'm picking at each boil.

God's ways are not my ways;
I thank the Lord for that.
I struggle with myself;
Legs cramped, I'm falling flat.

And since I cannot walk
To where I itch to go,
It saves me from the snares;
I'm able to say no.
There's swelling everywhere;
This abscess deeper digs.
I writhe in misery.
Where is my balm of figs?

When I reach out to God
What's cloudy He makes clear.
When idols are removed
It's then He'll reappear.

No need to raise my wrongs
And let my mind replay.
When I repent of sins
They're dead. God lets them lay.
I let go of this world,
Its spiritual rejection,
And I pick up my cross;
He offers me perfection.

He healed me with His love
Like no one could before.
And though He's done enough,
He's steadfast to do more.

Count Blessings, Not Flies

In beehive hair and flypaper dress
I'm armed with cans of pesticide.
I seek his legions to arrest;
The lord of flies is sly to hide.

His maggots are lured by the trash
I've been collecting since the fall.
Rolled newspapers like swatters held,
But I miss them and smack the wall.

I've got to take my garbage out;
I cannot hoard what's decomposed.
Must shoo these dragons off my fruit,
Make sure screen doors and souls stay closed.

Why fear their curse with all You've done?
The land of Goshen You protect.
These sores, to You, mere swarms of dust,
And yet Your love I still suspect.

My problems seem unbeatable;
I'm weighed down by my heavy lack.
Although my taxing load is like
A fly upon Your chiseled back.

If I could move into the space
To count the blessings, not the flies,
I'd be aware of God's sole view,
Not buying lies from compound eyes.

Self-pity, fear would then buzz off;
Instead, I would remain tried-true,
Acknowledging that each good thing
Including life has come from You.

If we could comprehend the great
Significance of what You've done,
Our sacrifice? Like filthy rags
Set side by side to sinless Son.

You are an awesome, mighty God;
Your skills are always on display.
Like sugar-water-vinegar
You catch each buzzing, whizzing stray.

So when we've ope'd our mouths to breathe
It's not these flies that fill our lungs.
Now throats are clear; we're apt to praise;
It bounces off unfettered tongues.

So now we've seen and must make known
That when we doubt, rail, or complain
It baits the flies to come and feast,
Invites them in to have free reign.

Beelzebub is just a pest;
He's not so terrible and great.
With You I don't need pest control,
Since You completely terminate.

Losing Your Lives-Talk

Problem
> *Prescription*

"Protect your slaves and cattle ,
Shelter them inside."
But heed God, I did not;
Because of me, they died.
> *When God gives a command*
> *Just trust Him and obey.*
> *Why suffer consequence*
> *That need not come your way?*

Not sure that God can help;
Look at my circumstance.
I stand here paralyzed,
No faith to take a chance.
> *But you must look to God*
> *Not what you're going through.*
> *Your mess won't solve itself;*
> *There's more that you could do.*

How can I do God's will?
It's not what Pharaoh taught.
These options don't make sense;
My thoughts are not His thoughts.
> *If you just do what's right*
> *You won't fear getting caught.*
> *You're subject to your choice*
> *If known by you or not.*

If I'd obeyed His Word
I'd have my flocks today.
I did what I thought best;
I starve in disarray.
> *A cover God provides*
> *For all who've taken heed.*
> *If covering you seek,*
> *Then trust Him with your seed.*

God promised. Do I think
That He would lie to me?
He blessed the Israelites.
Is there some left for me?
> *He's not a partial God*
> *Who favors certain groups.*
> *Those following His laws*
> *We're blessed and we recoup.*

But I still have these needs;
Perhaps there's not enough.
God said, "Try Me in this."
I may just call His bluff.
> *If you need more, sow more;*
> *God's Word is without lack.*
> *It will, says Malachi,*
> *Increase what you get back.*

He owns the stock-filled hills.
I hoard whatev' I earn.
Too scared to trust and give.
All sowers get return?
> *Each treasure in the world*
> *He gladly wants to share.*
> *The bays of Heav'n do ope'*
> *To those who are His heir.*

The Spider and the Cobwebs

Just squash the spider! He's the cause of
trouble.
It's time we quit existing in a bubble.
If life has cobwebs in each corner now,
It won't for long, because I'll show you how—

To rid your home so he will not come back.
Through prayer we carefully plan our
attack.
Combat the evil one, not physically;
Our battle's not against humanity.

All things are possible when God's put first;
For starters, you must bless those whom you've
cursed.
These tangled webs are holding you like prey;
The spider saves you for a rainy day.

If you debug your life the way God taught,
Within these sticky threads you won't get
caught.
The spider hides inside the lies he's spun.
Arachnid's sneak attacks will leave you
stunned.

He'll spit his venom and digestive juice.
When paralyzed, he'll do his worst
abuse.
Don't get too comfy while you're wrapped in silk;
He'll bite, then drink your liquid flesh like milk.

To live, you must do all that God requires.
Before you're caught, get out your broom and
pliers.
Then sweep down webs, and don't let them grow
wider,
And use your tool to finally squash the
spider!

P.U.S.H.

I cannot push with paltry strength.
    This weather is extreme
If I'm not safe, surrendered, sound,
    Prostrate to the Supreme.

This hail keeps on bombarding me;
    It pelts until I yield.
I crumble underneath its strain
    If faith is not my shield.

It won't relent. Where can I hide
    When thund'rous lightning stalks?
This hooligan of ice hits me;
    It kills my folks and flock.

Regret like trees struck down on me;
    There is no way to breathe.
This pressure presses down on me;
    It's daunting; it won't leave!

This bark stares back; I'm trapped and damp;
    It's more than time to pray.
Obedience and prayer protect;
    It keeps the loss away.

Won't judge or beat myself to pulp
    When Satan shows my shame.
If counting failures, I can't move;
    I'm cold and soaked in blame.

If pelt by hail in my own mind,
      One thing could set me free:
To pray with great intensity,
      Like all depends on me.

Speak out my prayers until storms cease;
      I'll keep my lips a-flappin'.
To splinter trees on top of me,
      I **P**ray **U**ntil **S**tuff **H**appens.

Your Momma Didn't Love You, and Your Daddy Didn't Care

Your momma didn't love you,
   and your daddy didn't care;
`Cause if he did, he would have come
   to rescue you from there.

Those daily beatings couldn't be stopped,
   curled in a ball too much;
So now you break relationships
   and flinch at every touch.

Mom said, "You're a mistake; you're bad,"
   no matter what you did.
You wondered why she hated you,
   since you were just a kid.

You tried your best defusing her;
   when sparked she was a bomb.
Most nights you cried yourself to sleep;
   you craved the love of Mom.

A mother always loves her child
   more than herself, they say;
But you found that untrue; you barely
   made it through each day.

A child forced to defend itself,
   a heavy load to haul.
You're sure deep down your dad loves you,
   so how come he won't call?

You don't think much of God,
      because He didn't hear your plea.
You were imprisoned; where was He
      to set the captive free?

Mom's words in hot rage scalded you;
      for refuge you would search.
Can't trust the God Mom touted
      when she'd beat you after church.

At last, Mom kicked you out
      when you had barely turned sixteen;
Hate-love, mistrust relationships,
      and nothing in between.

You feel men are superior,
      protected by your pride;
So you use women and when done,
      like trash, they're tossed aside.

You wander city streets without a place
      to lay your head;
Perhaps your mom was right when she yelled,
      "You'd be better dead!"

Yet that was not God's path for you;
      no, that was not His plan.
But people disobey His word;
      He gave free will to man.

No, she didn't raise you like He would;
      His ways are not to shove.
No matter how you have behaved,
      He won't withdraw His love.

He won't insult or curse you—He'll affirm;
    He'll bless; He'll give.
Your future can be great; the past
    is one you can outlive.

Now open up your heart, and He'll repair
    the damage done.
He'll be your perfect Parent,
    since it felt like you had none.

He'll comfort you and wipe your tears;
    there is no need to guess—
The love He feels for you is more
    than words on Earth express.

All Hell's Come Against Me

When I was self-consumed,
I never had a foe;
But when I do God's will,
I'm swarmed each place I go.

When I leave my own mess
To help my friends with theirs,
That's when I get chased home
By West Nile Virus scares.

When I have sympathy,
And bleed to help the lost,
Blood suckers hunt me down;
They needle and accost.

Their colonies do feast
On human and on beast.
Their numbers have increased;
I need a last-rites priest.

These aches and this malaise
Won't thrive in thwarting me,
Nor these anopheles
Or principality.

Won't let malaria
Avert me from God's will.
No bouts of nausea
Will slow or keep me still.

My God won't let me down;
Each promise He has kept.
He knows the pain I feel
Because He even wept!

My end days will be spent
Removing stagnant wet
And bringing others in
The Lord's mosquito net.

Yes, God is my repellent;
He's present in these rooms.
He keeps these pests away
With citronella fumes.

Magicians have all failed,
Their powers no Rx.
They finally must admit
They can't cure, only vex.

Now insects are in check,
My tears no longer shed.
I've traded being weak
And seized His strength instead.

I'll show those bent for Hell
That they're on Satan's route.
So God can save their souls,
I'll help them to move out.

I'm here to plunder Hell,
Take captives by the load;
Then God will relocate them
To a heavenly ZIP Code.

Now it's a compliment
When Satan picks on me.
I must fill him with fear
That I'll make history.

If Satan sends his hordes
Of sandflies out to play,
They lose their urge to suck
Each time I kneel to pray.

Wake Up, You Walking Dead

Now blast alarms so I awake;
Protect my skin on every limb.
Not caught off guard by walking dead
Athirst to gnaw on fleshly whim.
The old-time saints had liveliness.
The Christians now are walking dead
Who live for weekends, work, and eat,
Then watch TV 'til time for bed.

When hungry, I'll consume God's Word;
No others best inoculate.
I won't feast on another's brain
And think their wisdom satiates.
Adept and agile with the truth,
I will not lumber with the herd.
I'll bring a spark of life back to
Lamebrains whose words have gotten slurred.

I want to help those prone to bites
Provide asylum from attack
And let their safety take first place;
If I am selfish, I'll draw back.
These zombies bitten by the world,
Their hopes and dreams died when they did.
When that contagion spreads throughout
It seems impossible to rid.

See, these corpse cannibals were once
Alive and human, they had names.
But when the virus spread, they conked;
Now they're but animated frames.

You can't get close; they have no sense,
No intellect or faith at work,
Just taste and smell, survival mode.
Your fragrance drives meat bags berserk.

Don't realize they're not alive
Until they see the healthy thrive.
Their impulse is to feed on you;
They bite in order to survive.
So if a part of you gets bit,
Then chop it off and hurl that part.
Best live without your vanity;
To keep a pathogen's not smart.

It's better living life while maimed
Than poisoning your body whole.
Because infection will consume,
Make rotting flesh acquire control.
When you are not absorbed with self
But with the Father's will instead,
You build up your immunity
And won't become the walking dead.

If biters chew on one you love,
They've suffered from a ghoul's intrusion.
There is a therapy that cures;
They'll need a holy blood transfusion.
When Christ's blood runs throughout their veins
Sinfections in them have to die.
So lead them to the Great Physician;
Watch the undead come alive!

ERADICATE

Time to Tent the House

Time to Tent the House

It's time to tent your house
If froggy thoughts have paralyzed.
They've filled your kneading bowls,
And in your bed's bullfrog surprise.
When toads are on your throne,
Their toxins drip on what you have.
You think it may be time
To smash in bits your golden calves?

When polliwogs invade
There usually is a cause.
Self-scrutiny's a must;
Don't jump from pad to pad, but pause.
In worship, draw near God;
Seek His forgiveness and be still.
With hearts contrite, hear Him;
Have eagerness to do His will.

Cry out, repent, believe;
Stretch forth your hands o'er all your dreams.
Command those frogs to leave,
And banish them back to the streams.
Don't hop back to the swamp
When they have been snuffed out in style.
Recall your slimy days
The place the croakers' corpses pile.

Be open, not bullheaded,
For that's where undue stress can start.
So when respite arrives
Don't puff with pride nor harden heart.

Haze Lifted

God gives amazing answers to my prayers.
My smoky mind's made clear
If I'd just set each trap He tells me to
    When mice with lice appear.

I could be living in the victory;
These mites won't stop my praise.
But sometimes pestilence will ravage me;
    Each bit of me they graze.

> *I let contaminated skin*
> *Remove my praise and steal my grin.*
> *Don't have to take it on the chin,*
> *When I could rise above this sin.*

Should I retaliate or search for cure?
I wash with tea tree oil.
Eradicate each louse, my motives pure,
    The arthropods will spoil.

God tells me how to make invasions cease;
He shows me when and where.
Now famine or a typhus outbreak can't
    Advance me to despair.

God vaccinates my spirit and my soul;
Haze lifted, I've new eyes.
No trouble on this earth can be compared
    To glory's future prize!

I'm Wide Awake

Insomnia
    Made me so tired
        That I would weep.
The boring drone
    Of Bible tracks
        Would make me sleep.
But that was then;
    I've been renewed
        Unlike before.
The Scriptures once
    Had been a bore;
        I now crave more.

I need insight.
    How can I get
        Enough of You?
Your Word resus-
    citates me when
        I face Code Blue!
I cannot wait
    To wake so we
        Can then unite.
You lifted bur-
    dens 'til they were
        So featherlight.

I must inhale,
    Read, hear, and live
        Your God-breathed Word;
No one's BS
    Or PhD's
        Will get me lured

Away from You.
>>No other voice
>>>>Is one I'll heed;
So strong my spi-
>>rit stands to shout
>>>>"It's all I need!"

I'll enter in
>>Your ample field
>>>>When time to graze.
Each time I feast,
>>Ingest Your truth,
>>>>You lift malaise.
I read Your Word
>>Then am revved up;
>>>>I can't count sheep.
Soon all assail-
>>ants facing me
>>>>You put to sleep.

Who needs caffeine?
>>The Word's my pep;
>>>>Unload more truth.
My heart commands
>>"Investigate!"
>>>>Now I'm a sleuth.
Your Word that once
>>Would zonk me out
>>>>If playing on repeat,
Ironically
>>Now has me charged,
>>>>Preventing me from sleep.

It Doesn't Have to Be This Grim

I want to demonstrate God's love;
I'm clumsy, where do I begin?
You're acting like I am diseased;
You leave, and heed familiar sin.

I end up being one who weeps,
Inept in what I aim to do.
I know God wants to nurse your wounds;
Compassion's thick He has for you.

And those God sends to speak to you
Have been intent to touch your heart.
But you won't let us get too close;
Your secret fear is we'll depart.

You're scared we will contaminate;
Bacterium spreads to your core.
But God came only to bring cures;
He wants divine health for you more.

You're angry and resenting God;
You feel that He's been awfully cruel.
Can't people see that He's been slack?
Should fill your lack, which you are due.

You won't give Him a chance to prove:
"Come try Me now; see that I'm good."
Since all the more He blesses you,
You still don't do the things you should.

You claim He treats you dreadfully,
As if He put Black Death on you.
And though He's sent so many friends
To clear the path for Him to you.

It never seems to be enough;
You're always wanting that much more.
The very blest's awaiting you;
He's knocking right outside your door!

You're dehydrated, parched; I know.
It doesn't have to be this grim.
He'll rehydrate your dry abode,
Insert IVs attached to Him.

I'll share the Word and pray for you
As would a sister that's in Christ.
But how else could He show His love?
He sent His Son to pay your price.

Miracles Need No Tricks

There's steady, sure, creative pow'r to heal;
    Allow God in the mix.
No remedies are in the smoke and mirrors;
    His miracles aren't tricks.

The proof's short legs grow long; the lame do walk
    And blind eyes are now ope'd
Not due to any medical advance
    Or raising one to hope.

For God so made our medicine today;
    It stems from His creation.
He'll use whatever means He thinks is best
    To order our vibrations.

I've friends who've had their healings verified;
    I know them personally.
And when they prayed, God's healing came—for AIDS,
    For cancer, and Hep C.

All tests confirmed the malady was there;
    Tests later, it was gone.
All pharmaceuticals have side effects;
    With God, it's pros, no cons.

Hey, skeptic, it was no false positive;
    Clean out your doubting mind.
The ultimate prescription for your health
    Will come from the Divine.

And even now, our God does miracles;
They're not of yesterday.
He's still the healer that He's always been,
And He's on call each day.

So if He's healed you, it's time to shout
To get the good news out,
So those with desperate need to be made well
Build faith, and drop their doubt.

Zach, the Good Boy

There was a good boy once,
A sailor boy named Zach
Who tragically fell prey
To a pirate's planned attack.
This mast of infiltration
Set his mind adrift;
No more full-speed ahead,
Torpedoes came too swift.

Zach couldn't cut and run;
The coxswain used such force.
Invasion of his fantail
Set his life off course.
He couldn't beat to quarters,
Or cry for help, "Ahoy!"
The good boy was now capsized,
Injected with bad boy.

No S.O.S. to save him
From these wicked wishes.
Instead of acting out,
He'd rather sleep with fishes.
Now tidal waves of thoughts
Had brought exciting fear;
He couldn't trust himself
If shipmates ventured near.

His sleep state was not deep;
He'd float awake in shoal.
On high alert to keep
A blitz at bay, his goal.

He kept the siege hush-hush,
But that brought no relief;
He could not get away,
Now snagged on coral reef.

Back home, he pet his cat
He yearned to split and gut;
Instead went to the bath,
With razor he would cut.
Had need to blow off steam,
For he was on the brink;
The basin filled with blood;
Red water's in the sink.

He wrapped a rag around
The arm that had been hurt;
He rinsed his bloodied blade
And donned a long-sleeve shirt.
And then he pondered why
His feelings were euphoric,
This pleasure numbed the prick;
For him it was historic.

Each night at supper time
His parents were ignored,
Not typical teen angst
Or due to being bored.
He had already planned
The next time he would cut;
No shrink could patch the hole
Or pull him from his rut.

He tried depression drugs;
He binged on food till stuffed,
And household chemicals
So frequently he huffed.
But nothing eased the ache,
Or lessened that grave weight.
The cargo bent his back
And aged the boy of eight.

"Hey, Zach, my boy, it's Ted.
Let's grab our poles and fish,"
Said by his favorite uncle.
This had been his wish!
The wind out there was calm,
The sunny day so fair.
They goofed off on the lake;
Ted tousled up Zach's hair.

Playtime got too personal;
This game did not feel right.
Zach's cheeks pierced by Ted's sword;
He's impotent to fight.
Zach screamed for liberty,
But there was no lifeboat.
He didn't have sea legs
For a voyage this remote.

Zach couldn't stop the siege,
Would drown without the bailer.
With each thrust on the ship,
He grew seasick and paler.

"Abandon ship! Walk the plank!"
Was all that he could think.
He jumped into the blue
Turned red; he prayed to sink.

A normal life had slipped
So swiftly down the stream.
Dad's voice awoke him from
A wet and dreadful dream.
"Should we play catch tonight?"
"No, thanks, Dad; that's okay."
Then Mom said, "Zach, what's wrong?
You're not yourself today."

The surface tension deep,
He searched for a solution.
His septic tank was full
Of water rats' pollution.
The silence deafened still,
What's left unsaid, not heard.
See, Zach once talked so much,
Now wouldn't say a word.

"You're such a bad boy, Zach,"
The voices wouldn't wane.
His constant bearing south,
His hope sloshed down the drain.
Though dying for discourse,
Words kept inside a vault;
His life a sour cesspool,
Convinced it was his fault.

So stagnant was his soul;
Could not communicate.
With no flow in or out,
Life docked, he harbored hate.
The fishing he outgrew,
His parents had assumed.
He bypassed family ties;
All friendships were marooned.

Poor Zach had been detained,
Yet his own mind the brig;
Careening all his plans,
Unwanted pirate frig.
His folks could not get through;
He stayed in disconnect.
He'd never sail again;
His childhood was shipwrecked.

Mom caught Zach watching films,
Astonishingly lewd;
Their ratings triple X,
She's mortified he viewed.
Entangled in new net,
Enticed by what he saw.
A safety-valve release,
Or hook inside his jaw?

"I'll talk to him," said Dad.
"Dear wife, no need to panic."
Zach bounced between despair
And hiding he was manic.

The school kids didn't know,
And yet they called him gay.
Word volleys cold and cruel
Wreaked havoc every day.

A new boy joined his class,
A beacon for attention.
Zach planned to perpetrate,
What he'd not dare to mention.
A victim Zach desired,
Now didn't need to search.
As Rock gave him an invite:
"Come sleep over after church."

Mom loved the thought of that;
She said, "It's awfully nice;
Zach finally made a friend."
He'd taken her advice.
And Zach thought, "Here's my chance;
I can't help that I'm bad."
All hands on deck won't stop
The strategy he had.

No matter what he'd tried
His life was black and bleak.
He couldn't catch his breath
No matter how he'd seek.
Compulsions to do wrong,
The devil's been let loose.
And he'd perpetuate
The cycle of abuse.

At church he'd play along,
But never would confess.
Arms folded and he scoffed,
"It's brainwashing B.S."
This "gospel" they've conveyed
Has got to be a lie.
Why would a perfect man
Be nailed for me, and die?

No way did this make sense,
Afraid to take that bait,
His heart a sunken chest
No one could excavate.
"If in captivity,"
They said, "You can be free.
Believe it in your heart,
And speak this prayer with me."

They laid hands on his heart,
And laid hands on his head.
Could he, at last, be free,
Not overpowered by dread?
A virgin to the power
Of God "slain in the Spirit";
Enclosed in light so bright,
And yet he did not fear it.

"My child," a strong voice called.
God gently spoke Zach's name.
"If you put trust in Me,
You'll never be the same.

To grow to be the man
I've destined you to be,
Cut anchors shaped from pain
And float yourself to Me."

Set free from prison hulk,
Renewed that very hour,
In God's life vest now dressed,
Tossed evil's drowning power.
As tears streamed down his face,
New life began to spring.
The Living Water's flood
Had cleansed, removed the sting.

Corruption he'd been through
Would rule his life no more.
The ocean spit him out;
A good boy washed ashore.
He hugged his new friend Rock,
Didn't leave him in the lurch.
With joy and freedom fresh,
He ran straight home from church.

He rushed his parents' room,
Absolved of former crime.
His folks would get him back;
`Twas restoration time.
He held his parents tight,
Said, "Thanks for being there."
Then bravely, said, "Mom, Dad...
There's something I must share..."

When Language Fails

The soul that cries out loud to God
Will never call in vain.
And those who put their trust in Him
Will never be the same.

The Lord will hear your prayer, and He's
The only one who saves.
His faithfulness is not a thing
That only comes in waves.
The Lord is God, and He forgives;
His mercy is enough.
His arm is not too short to save
In circumstances rough.

When you call out God's name, you don't
Just say the syllables.
But have Him cap your emptiness—
He makes you fillable.

If Jesus dwells in you, that's where
He chooses to abide.
So speak His name; it builds your faith
And fills in sin's divide.
We don't have to be formal in
Our opening or close.
Our prayers need not be poetry;
He's happy with our prose.

God's name to open prayer's a start
But likewise in our seal,
He gave us His authority;
Our faith will close the deal.

Despite our depth of love for God
All earthly language fails.
But uttering our Savior's name
Repeatedly's not stale.
If you have heard your child awake
In panic just to shriek
Your name into the dark of night,
What is there left to speak?

For that had far more power than
Appeals with many words
So, too, when crying out to God,
Our calls are always heard.

Rising Up

Do you feel anger rising up?
What gets you steaming mad?
It's time to make a list;
Get out your pen and pad.
What are all the injustices
That fully set you off?
Discover every one.
Pray tell, what makes you wroth?

Is it domestic violence?
Children who are beaten?
Graffiti on the walls?
The homeless who've not eaten?
Is it the elderly defrauded?
Or snuffed out pre-born life?
Those nations starved by drought?
Internet scams? Gang strife?

Or how the government is run?
Civil rights? Gendercide?
Humans being trafficked?
Or Veterans' suicide?
Is it all that unhealthy grub
They've marketed to kids?
Or just to find an easy way
To pop off stubborn lids?

So if you're livid, what's the cause?
How can it be resolved?
You'll find in life your mission tied
To problems you want solved.

I Will Prevail

I thought I couldn't make life work,
But that was just a lie
That Satan told me from his pit
With his perverse reply.

All things are possible with God;
No thing can be restrained.
His bondage dropped off me, and God's
Inheritance was gained.

The signs I've seen have changed my life;
He kept me from each plague.
God's ever clear with His instructions;
Never is He vague.

Since He gave me the mind of Christ
To awe and fear the Lord
I've supernatural judgment too;
The Spirit has outpoured.

I've no more thoughts that I will fail,
Nor any of defeat.
I took them to the cross and laid
Them at my Savior's feet.

There's nothing I can do myself
When foes have gained on me.
Yet all God wants is me to trust
He'll part the big Red Sea.

I'll make it to the other side
And there awaits my crown.
Not only will I get my prize,
My enemies will drown.

So, Satan, keep your idle threats;
He crushed you long ago.
God gave authority to me
I order you to go.

In Jesus' name, I say to you,
Foul spirit, you must flee.
I will continue, and prevail
In all God has for me!

Afterword

I hope you have enjoyed *Poetic Prescriptions for Plaguing Problems: Biblical Remedies for When Life Bites*. I have to tell you that many years of work went into the making of this, as well as careful thought and heartache. But it was also fun when I was able to capture in a visual, uplifting, sometimes heart-wrenching way how to be victorious when life's trials bombard.

When I had written the first couple of books, I got a lot of great feedback telling me that I should keep writing, keep making these prescription books told through an entertaining medium. I didn't know the impact they were making until I had more than a couple of people let me know they were thinking about ending their life because they were so hopeless and overwhelmed with their problems, but then they read my book and decided to make life work. You can imagine that was very humbling, and it was a great motivator to keep putting these solutions out there.

Please leave a review on whichever website you purchased the book from.

Thank you so much for reading *Poetic Prescriptions* and for spending time with me.

In gratitude,

Katherine Norland

The information contained in these books is not intended to be a substitute for professional, medical, or psychological advice. It is strictly anecdotal, provided for inspirational and entertainment purposes only. You assume full responsibility for how you choose to use this information.

Other books by the author:

Poetic Prescriptions for Eternal Youth: Examining Earthly Beauty from a Heavenly Perspective

Katherine Norland picks apart societal standards of beauty that have been foisted upon us. She shatters misconceptions about image and self-worth in this truthful yet lighthearted look at our bodies, and the difference a divine perspective makes.

In *Poetic Prescriptions for Eternal Youth,* Katherine pops the fallacy of perfection like a ripe zit. And like a squishy muffin top over designer jeans a size or two too small, she lets her true self hang over the tight constraints of the media's portrayal of sexiness.

Exposing her own foibles as a young woman seeking to attain the images she was bombarded with in magazines, she delves into the ridiculousness of trying to look like Barbie's twin. Then she moves through the dread of aging, where you no longer recognize yourself in the mirror, to finally embracing the journey—cracks and all.

Although her self-esteem had been crushed like peanut shells at the corner bar, the transformation she found didn't come from a Beverly Hills surgeon but instead from a shift in her perspective. She realized that a lasting makeover is not attained by starving yourself slim, Botoxing your brains out, or buying a Brazilian butt. Instead of finding comfort in a candy bar, she began to examine earthly beauty through God's eyes, and in this book, she uncovers the real way to gain eternal youth.

Poetic Prescriptions for Pesky Problems

In today's fast-paced, busy life, we are constantly being bombarded with so-called "cures for what ails you!" Most of these quick fixes are nothing more than mere placebos.

Life on Earth can be daunting at times, but there is an accepted "prescription" for the suffering and the challenges of life we face on a daily basis, and it can be found in the scriptures: the Word of God.

Poetic Prescriptions for Pesky Problems unleashes truth in a manner that can be easily understood, with sensitivity and even a bit of irony. It is a prescription that can be taken PRN, i.e., whenever necessary!

Katherine's insight and candor are refreshing because she goes directly to the heart of the matter. Take no offense to her in-your-face handling of the issue or situation she is confronting, as she points the way out, which scriptural inspiration has directed her to map out before you.

53765393R00061

Made in the
USA
Lexington, KY